BOWLING

THIRD EDITION

Richard T. Mackey

Miami University
Oxford, Ohio

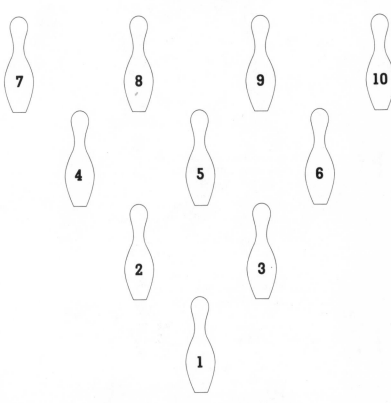

Mayfield Publishing Company

Library of Congress Catalog Number: 80-82563
International Standard Book Number: 0-87484-513-0

Manufactured in the United States of America
Mayfield Publishing Company
285 Hamilton Avenue, Palo Alto, California 94301

Compositor: Acme Type Company
Printer and binder: Malloy Lithography
Sponsoring editor: C. Lansing Hays
Managing editor: Maggie Cutler
Manuscript editor: Jay Stewart
Designer: Nancy Sears
Layout: Mary Wiley
Production: Michelle Hogan

CONTENTS

1

YOUR APPROACH
TO BOWLING

What do you need to enjoy bowling? At the rate new bowlers are joining the devotees, a place to bowl might seem to be the prime necessity for bowling fun these days. It is a fact, however, that people feel satisfied when they do things with a degree of success. And what are the ingredients of successful bowling— the things that increase your enjoyment? Certainly your attitude toward the sport is important. Bowling is basically a game of finesse rather than power. It is true that hurling the ball with tremendous speed and seeing the pins splatter can be a pleasure, but the satisfaction of consistent good performance comes with controlled speed. Although you can see much variation in the styles of top-notch bowlers, certain similarities will also be evident. Good bowlers are smooth bowlers, and they have a flowing motion as they approach the foul line and deliver the ball. Accomplished bowlers also have the good balance essential to outstanding performance. Besides the physical or mechanical aspects of the skill, there is the mental side of bowling. Poise and confidence based upon sound techniques are important. The

1

development of these factors will increase your own enjoyment of America's number one indoor sport.

May this book contribute to both your bowling skill and pleasure.

A BRIEF HISTORY OF BOWLING

The urge to throw a stone or a similar pellet at an object is basic to the play habits of people throughout the world, so it is not surprising to find the historical accounts of bowling going back seven thousand years. The Egyptians played a game similar to modern tenpins in 5200 B.C. According to some historians, bowling was introduced into Europe in 50 B.C. via the Italian game that has come to be known as *boccie*. And no history of the sport would be complete without mentioning the contribution of Wilhelm Pehle, a member of the German Bowling Society and Berlin Bowling Club. Pehle was a great student of the game who indicated in his book, *Bowling*, written in the nineteenth century that religion and bowling were closely associated as far back as the fourth century A.D. At that time bowling was done in the cathedrals as a religious ceremony. The parishioners were asked to place their pins or *kegels* at the end of the cloister and then were given a round stone called a *heide* ("*heathen*"). If the *kegler* was successful in knocking over his pin, this indicated a clean and pure life. Failure to knock over the pin called for

3

stricter adherence to church rules and regulations.

As time went on, changes in both the equipment and rules took place. Specially shaped pins were developed, small stones were replaced by larger ones, and wooden balls were eventually substituted for stones. The game lost its religious significance, but it continued to be played by the upper class of laymen rather than by the common man. Martin Luther was an avid bowler and established the ninepin game that became standard in Germany. The game of bowling spread from Germany into Belgium, Holland, and Austria in the fifteenth, sixteenth and seventeenth centuries. Skittles, as bowling was called in England, was introduced there in the fourteenth century. Lawn bowling, a present-day favorite of the British, had its beginning with the development of skittles.

The Dutch are credited with bringing bowling to the United States. It is not known just when this happened, but the year 1820 is accepted by most bowling historians. By 1835 bowling at pins gained considerable popularity in the area of New York, New England, and as far south as Washington, D.C. Unfortunately, gamblers also began to take a keen interest in bowling, and in a few years they just about took over the sport. Conditions became so bad that in 1841 the Connecticut state legislature passed an act prohibiting "bowling at 9 pins," which was the standard game then. The legislative action, however, did not preclude the formation of the game of tenpins. A group of men who wanted to continue the sport without the gambling developed this new game and met to establish rules for its conduct. This meeting, which took place in 1895, marked the organization of the American Bowling Congress (ABC) and so established the group that was to shape the

game as we know it today. In 1901 the ABC conducted its first national championship tournament
in Chicago. These tournaments have continued
through the years since than and have gained a large
following. By 1942 ABC members numbered more
than a million, and by 1961 membership exceeded
the 4 million mark. The number of ABC members
for 1978 was over 4.7 million. The membership of the
Women's International Bowling Congress (WIBC),
which was founded in 1916 in St. Louis, Missouri,
also passed the 4 million mark in 1978.

Among professional bowlers, the prizes have
shown a similar increase. On January 2, 1961, the
biggest single bowling prize to date was won by Ther-
man Gibson of Detroit; he won $78,000 on the Jack-
pot Bowling television show, and he picked up this
huge amount by rolling six straight strikes.

Dick Weber of St. Louis occupied a unique place
in bowling history for the period from 1959 to 1965.
During that time he averaged $36,000 per year in
tournament winnings, with a total for the period of
more than $225,000. This amount was more than
double that of his nearest competitor. But then, con-
trast that with the earnings of Mark Roth of North
Arlington, New Jersey, who set a new record for winnings in one year with a $134,850 total in 1978.

In noting the growth of the sport in terms of the
number of ABC and WIBC members, it must be re-
membered that the memberships of these groups
represent only a fraction of the total number who
bowl. The most remarkable growth in the sport has
taken place since 1954. Automatic pinsetters as well
as lavish bowling establishments complete with free
baby-sitting service, free lunches, and free lessons
have made the sport attractive to the entire family. In
their highly successful efforts to eradicate the stigma

of the past, bowling promoters now refer to the bowling surface as *lanes* rather than alleys. In 1954 there were seventeen million bowlers in the United States. In 1978 the estimated number was sixty million, and whether this represents peak participation is anybody's guess.

SOME IMPORTANT DATES
IN THE HISTORY OF BOWLING

5200 B.C.	Egyptians engaged in a game similar to modern tenpins.
50 B.C.	Bowling introduced into Europe.
300 A.D.	Bowling or *kegeling* became a part of the religious activities in Germany.
1300	Skittles, a forerunner of lawn bowling, was introduced in England.
1820	Bowling introduced in the United States by the Dutch.
1841	Connecticut state legislature passed an act prohibiting "bowling at 9 pins."
1895	American Bowling Congress established.
1901	First national tournament conducted by the American Bowling Congress.
1916	Woman's International Bowling Congress organized.
1932	Bowling Proprietors Association of America established.
1952	ABC first approved use of automatic pinsetters.
1954	Total number of bowlers in United States estimated at 17 million.
1962	ABC approved an all-synthetic bowling

pin, the first nonwood pin found acceptable.

1966   ABC and WIBC established collegiate divisions.

1978   Total number of bowlers in the United States estimated at 60 million.

1978   ABC approved twenty-five hundredth 300 game.

SOME FAMOUS MEN IN AMERICAN BOWLING

James Blouin — American Bowling Congress All Events Champion, 1909. ABC Singles Winner, 1911. Elected to ABC Hall of Fame, 1953.

Henry Marino — Compiled 190 average during forty-six years of competing in ABC tournaments. ABC Doubles Champion, 1916. Included among those elected to ABC Hall of Fame at its inception in 1941.

Andy Varipapa — Colorful trick bowler and outstanding competitor. Named to ABC Hall of Fame, 1957.

Ned Day — Maintained 202 average in ABC competition, 1940. Elected to ABC Hall of Fame, 1952. ABC All Events Individual Champion, 1948.

Billy Sixty — Active in ABC bowling competition for over forty years. Writer of books and articles on the sport. Member of ABC All Events Team Champions, 1948. Elected to ABC Hall of Fame, 1961.

Outstanding Modern Bowlers

Some outstanding bowlers in the modern era, many of whom have been honored as members of *Bowling Magazine's* All-American Team, are listed below. The group includes ABC Tournament Champions, ABC Masters Tournament Champions, and Bowling Proprietors Association of America Tournament Champions. Although chosen without regard to geographical origin, they are grouped here by sections of the country.

East

Lou Campi, Dumont, New Jersey
Al Faragalli, Wayne, New Jersey
Fred Lening, Yardley, Pennsylvania
Junie McMahon, River Edge, New Jersey
Andy Varipapa, Hempstead, New Jersey

Midwest

Ray Bluth, St. Louis, Missouri
Nelson Burton, Jr., St. Louis, Missouri
Don Carter, St. Louis, Missouri
Tom Hennessey, St. Louis, Missouri
Dick Hoover, Akron, Ohio
Jim Stefanich, Joliet, Illinois
Dick Weber, St. Louis, Missouri
Billy Welu, St. Louis, Missouri

South

Bill Allen, Orlando, Florida
Billy Hardwick, Louisville, Kentucky
Bill Lillard, Dallas, Texas
Wayne Zahn, Atlanta, Georgia

West

Glenn Allison, Los Angeles, California

Dave Davis, Phoenix, Arizona
Andy Marzich, Torrance, California
Norm Meyers, Los Angeles, California
Jim St. John, Santa Clara, California

1979 All-American Teams

First team
Earl Anthony, Tacoma, Washington
Nelson Burton, Jr., St. Louis, Missouri
Marshall Holman, Medford, Oregon
Tommy Hudson, Akron, Ohio
Mark Roth, North Arlington, New Jersey

Second team
Dave Davis, Hackensack, New Jersey
Larry Laub, San Francisco, California
Jeff Mattingly, Tacoma, Washington
George Pappas, Charlotte, North Carolina
Johnny Petraglia, Staten Island, New York

SOME FAMOUS WOMEN IN AMERICAN BOWLING

Women have also achieved fame in this sport. Both outstanding service and athletic achievement are represented in the three-category Hall of Fame of the WIBC, which has honored women bowlers since 1953. The Stars of Yesteryear section of the honor group recognizes bowling achievement, including at least one WIBC title, while the Meritorious Service Award recognizes service that is not necessarily dependent on bowling prowess. The Superior Performance Award honors current individual bowling success.

The best woman bowler of the modern era and

perhaps of all time is Marion Ladewig. She retired from major competition on December 14, 1964, at the age of fifty, but the accomplishments of this bowling grandmother are almost beyond belief. They include eight All-Star titles in fifteen years, five World's Invitational crowns in eight years, and numerous other championships. She dominated women's bowling for more than fifteen years.

WIBC Roster of the Greats

Superior performance

1964
Marion Ladewig, Grand Rapids, Michigan

1966
Sylvia Wene Martin, Philadelphia, Pennsylvania

1970
Helen Duval, Berkeley, California

1971
Shirley Garms, Chicago, Illinois

1972
Beverly Ortner, Tucson, Arizona

1974
Joan Holm, Chicago, Illinois

1975
Mildred Martorella, Rochester, New York

1976
Judy Soutar, Kansas City, Missouri
Doris Coburn, Buffalo, New York

1977
LaVerne Carter, St. Louis, Missouri

1978
Mae Bolt, Chicago, Illinois
Pat Dryer, Indianapolis, Indiana

Stars of Yesteryear

1953
Emma Jaeger, Toledo, Ohio
Grayce Garwood Hatch, Cleveland, Ohio
Goldie Greenwald, Cleveland, Ohio
Louise Stockdale, Los Angeles, California

1954
Dorothy Miller, Chicago, Illinois
Marie Warmbier, Chicago, Illinois

1955
Philena Bolen, Los Angeles, California

1956
Floretta McCutcheon, Los Angeles, California

1957
Emily Chapman, New York, New York

1958
Catherine Burling, Cincinnati, Ohio

1959
Jo Mraz, Cleveland, Ohio

1960
Violet Simon, San Antonio, Texas

1961
Addie Ruschmeyer, New York, New York

1962
Anita Rump, Fort Wayne, Indiana

1963
Esther Ryan, Milwaukee, Wisconsin

1964
Sally Twyford, Indianapolis, Indiana

1965
Myrtle Schulte, St. Louis, Missouri

1966
Deane Fritz, Toledo, Ohio
1967
Madalene (Bee) Hochstadter, Chicago, Illinois
1968
Grace Smith, Albuquerque, New Mexico
1969
Leona Robinson, Los Angeles, California
1970
Catherine Fellmeth, Chicago, Illinois
1971
Tess Morris Small, Chicago, Illinois
1972
Stella Hartrick, Detroit, Michigan
1973
Connie Powers, Detroit, Michigan
1974
Merle Matthews, Los Angeles, California
1975
Cecelia Winandy, Chicago, Illinois
1976
Olga Gloor, Chicago, Illinois
Elvira Toepfer, Detroit, Michigan
1977
Helen Shablis, Detroit, Michigan
Nina Van Camp Burns, Chicago, Illinois

Meritorious service
1963
Jeannette Knepprath, Milwaukee, Wisconsin
1964
Nora Kay, Toledo, Ohio

1965
Emma Phaler, Columbus, Ohio
1966
Berdie Speck, St. Louis, Missouri
1967
Iolia Lasher, Albany, New York
1968
Bertha McBride, St. Paul, Minnesota
1969
Margaret Higley, San Jose, California
1970
Ann Wood, Cincinnati, Ohio
1972
Gertrude Rishling, Omaha, Nebraska
1973
Pearl Switzer, South Bend, Indiana
1974
Georgia E. Veatch, Chicago, Illinois
1975
Mildred White, Rockford, Illinois
1976
Winfred Berger, San Francisco, California
1977
Helen Baetz, San Antonio, Texas
Dorothy Haas, Perth Amboy, New Jersey
1978
Theresa Kelone, Little Rock, Arkansas

3

THE ETIQUETTE
OF BOWLING

To completely enjoy bowling, you will feel more confident with some know-how of the generally accepted proper conduct. These rules are based on common courtesy and can be mastered easily with just a little thought. The fundamental idea is to treat others with courtesy and consideration, as you would like to be treated. This makes the game more enjoyable for everyone playing. The following are some of the more important guides to good bowling manners:

1. Check the number of the ball you have selected and use your own ball each time. It is annoying to have to wait because another bowler is using your ball.

2. Generally, you should let the bowler to your right bowl first if you are both ready at the same time. (An exception occurs when you are bowling your second ball and he is rolling his first in that frame.) When it is not your turn, stay off the approach. Also step back and off the approach after making each delivery.

3. Be ready to bowl when it is your turn. Slowing the play, especially when you're bowling on a team, can be annoying to everyone.

4. A little "needling" may be part of the fun of bowling, but avoid doing it after the other person has addressed the pins.

5. Keep refreshments away from the bench and the bowling area. A spot of soft drink on the bottom of a bowling shoe can cause a nasty fall.

6. Put your bowling shoes on before you select your bowling ball. Dirt from your street shoes should not be carried onto the lanes.

7. Control your temper. All of us experience disappointment at a missed strike or spare, but kicking the ball rack or using profanity is strictly taboo.

8. Do not "loft" the ball. This is not good bowling technique, and it damages the lanes.

9. When you win, enjoy it, but when you lose, don't detract from the other person's success.

10. Observe the foul line. When you foul, you lose any pins you have knocked down.

11. Limit your body movements to your own lane. Don't let your body twist after you release the ball so an arm or leg extends into an adjacent lane. It is poor follow-through technique and can be very distracting to another bowler.

4

BOWLING TERMS

Anchor Man   The last man in the line-up of a team.

Approach   The area the bowler takes her or his steps on prior to delivering the ball at the foul line.

Baby Split   The 2–7 or 3–10 split.

Backup   A ball that curves left to right for a right-hander, right to left for a left-hander.

Bedposts   The 7–10 split.

Blind   Score given a team for an absent member.

Blow   Failing to make a spare except in the case of a split that cannot normally be made. Also called an *error* or a *miss*.

Board   One of the one-inch boards making up each lane.

Brooklyn Hit   A ball that rolls into the pocket on the wrong side of the head pin. Also called a *crossover* or *Jersey* hit.

Channel   A more modern term for the gutter.

Cherry   *See* Chop.

Chop   Knocking down the front pin on a spare attempt, leaving adjacent pins standing. Also referred to as a *cherry*.

Convert   When you successfully make your spare.

Creeper   A very slow ball.

Crossover   *See* Brooklyn hit.

Curve   A ball that has a wide and sweeping arc, more pronounced than a hook.

Dead Ball   A poorly rolled ball which has little action—doesn't take down as many pins as a "live" ball.

Double   Two strikes in succession.

Error   A blow or miss.

Fast Lanes   A lane on which the hook ball does not curve or "take" as much as usual.

Foul   Touching or going beyond the foul line when the bowler delivers the ball.

Foul Line   The line that separates the approach from the lane.

Frame   The box on the scoresheet in which the score is recorded; also one-tenth of a game.

Gutterball   A ball that goes off the lane into the gutter.

Handicap   A means of enabling individuals or teams of different averages to compete in the same league.

Head Pin   The 1 pin, which is the pin closest to the bowler.

Hook   A ball that breaks to the left for a right-hander or to the right for a left-hander.

Kegler   A synonym for bowler, derived from the German word *kegel.*

Kingpin   The 5 pin.

Lane   A synonym for alley.

Leadoff person   The first bowler in a team line-up.

Leave The pins remaining standing after the first ball is rolled in a frame.

Line A game of ten frames.

Lofting Throwing the ball too far out on the lane so that it bounces.

Mark A strike or spare.

Open Frames A frame without a strike or a spare.

Pin Bowling Using the pins as aiming points.

Pocket The area defined by the 1–3 pins for right-handers; the 1–2 for left-handers.

Railroad *See* split.

Scratch Bowler A bowler who has no handicap.

Sleeper A pin hidden behind another pin.

Span Distance between thumbhole and finger holes.

Spare Knocking down all ten pins with two balls in a frame.

Split A leave in which the head pin is down and two or more pins remain standing with adjacent pins knocked down in front and between; also known as a *railroad*.

Spot Bowling Using the range finders or spots as aiming points.

Strike Knocking down all pins with the first ball.

Strike Out To get three strikes in the tenth and final frame.

Sweeper A live ball that sweeps the pins off the lane.

Tap Leaving a 10, 4, or 7 pin on what appeared to be a strike ball.

Turkey Three strikes in a row.

Washout The 1–2–4–10 leave for a right-hander; the 1–3–6–7 leave for a left-hander.

5

TIPS FOR BEGINNERS

When you visit a bowling establishment, you'll notice almost as many different styles and techniques as there are bowlers. Even among experts, individual refinements will vary a lot, although there will be some basic similarities. Certain questions may occur to you: How do I select a ball? Should I use a three-, four-, or five-step delivery? Is a hook better than a straight ball? When you listen to the conversation of bowlers, you may become even more confused by hearing such terms as *spot bowling, pin bowling, backup ball,* and *curve.* The following section is designed to eliminate some of this confusion and to provide you with some guidelines for a good start at learning the skills of bowling.

SELECTING YOUR BALL

The weight of a bowling ball varies from 8 to 16 pounds, as determined by the rules of American Bowling Congress. Most men use the 16-pound ball, although a lighter ball is recommended if you have difficulty with control. Most women definitely improve their accuracy using a lighter ball. Here is the specific technique by which to select your ball (see Figure 1):

Your thumb should slip in and out of the thumbhole rather easily.

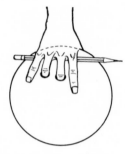

There ought to be just enough space under your palm for a pencil to fit snugly.

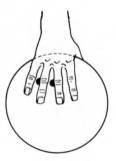

For proper span, the knuckles of your middle fingers should be over the edges of the finger holes with your thumb in the thumbhole.

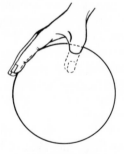

Only by actually using the ball can you determine whether the fit is correct.

FIGURE 1
SELECTING YOUR BALL

First, make sure your thumb will slip in and out of the thumbhole easily. Second, with your thumb in the thumbhole, lay your hand across the ball but do not put your fingers into the finger holes. The knuckles of your middle two fingers should be directly over the inside edge of the finger holes. When you insert the thumb and the two middle fingers into the holes, there should be just enough space between your palm and the ball for a pencil to fit snugly. This is the simplest way to determine the correct span. If you purchase your own ball, your bowling proprietor will take more exact measurements. There's no doubt that having your own properly fitted ball is a definite asset in developing consistency.

THREE-, FOUR-, OR FIVE-STEP APPROACH

All three types of delivery are being used with effectiveness; however, the four-step delivery is suggested for beginners, as well as for more advanced bowlers (see chapter 6). It is smoother, provides better balance than the three-step variety, and is less complicated than the five-step delivery.

THE STRAIGHT BALL
VERSUS THE HOOK BALL,
THE CURVE, OR THE BACKUP

The straight ball is delivered from a position toward the right side of the approach directly into the 1–3 pocket (see figure 2). It has no sideward spin and so does not curve to the left or right. It is probably the most easily controlled of the group, but most bowling authorities recommend the hook ball, even for beginners. The spot bowling system presented in chapter 6 applies to both straight and hook balls.

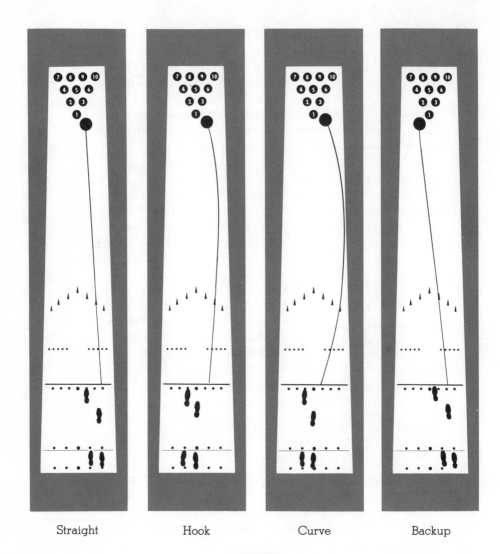

FIGURE 2
TYPES OF DELIVERY

Note: Drawings not to scale.

The hook ball and the curve ball, when delivered properly, provide better action (knock down more pins) than the straight ball. To roll a hook, the ball is released with the hand in a handshake position. This puts a counterclockwise spin on the ball, causing it to curve left. (For left-handers, of course, the directions are reversed.) Your instructor will help you decide if you are ready to learn the hook delivery. It may be that you will show a natural hook right from the start of instruction, or your instructor may prefer that you start out with the hook rather than a straight ball. More detailed information about the hook ball is included in chapter 11, "Tips for Advanced Bowlers."

The backup ball is the result of either faulty delivery or a natural tendency to throw a ball that curves left to right. Some people have a natural backup ball. Faults that cause this include turning the hand in a clockwise manner as the ball is released or pulling the hand up and to the right in the follow-through. Your instructor can help you decide whether your backup ball is natural and reasonably effective or whether it needs correcting. It is true that the left-to-right curve can produce good action, but only when consistency of delivery can be attained.

Figure 3 illustrates the hand positions at the moment of release for the straight, hook, curve, and backup balls. Note that the position of the thumb for the straight ball is at twelve o'clock, while the ring finger of the right hand points to six o'clock. The hand is rotated to the left for the hook, with the thumb at ten o'clock and the ring finger at four o'clock. Thus, to progress from a straight ball to a slight hook, the thumb is positioned at eleven o'clock and the ring finger at five o'clock. Additional rotation to the left creates the curve hand position. The thumb is at nine o'clock and the ring finger at three o'clock. Finally, the backup hand position finds the thumb at one o'clock and the third finger at seven o'clock.

FAST LANES

A fast lane is one on which your hook ball does not curve or take as much as usual. The lessened curve is caused by a lack of friction that reduces the sideward spin of the ball. A highly polished, glassy surface may be your tip-off to a fast lane, but you won't really know until you have thrown a few balls. If your ball misses the 1–3 pocket to the right on each practice roll, you should move slightly to the right of your usual starting position. As chapter 7 on spot bowling explains, this will shift the path of your ball slightly to the left.

SLOW LANES

If, on your practice rolls, your ball curves to the left of the 1–3 pocket and hits pins to the left of the head pin, you may be on a slow lane. Increased friction on the lane causes an exaggeration of your hook ball. Dust on your ball or on the lanes could also cause a slow-lane condition. Move slightly to the left of your normal starting position to make the necessary adjustment.

SPEED AND BALL WEIGHT
AS THEY AFFECT PIN ACTION

The two factors relating to the action that results when your ball hits the pins are the speed and weight of your ball. High-speed photography has shown that the extremely fast ball lifts the pins vertically and

 Straight

Thumb at twelve o'clock;
ring finger at six o'clock.

 Hook

Thumb at ten o'clock;
ring finger at four o'clock.

 Curve

Thumb at nine o'clock;
ring finger at three o'clock.

 Backup

Thumb at one o'clock;
ring finger at seven o'clock.

FIGURE 3
HAND POSITIONS FOR DIFFERENT DELIVERIES

therefore reduces pin action. The ball delivered with moderate speed causes the front pins to fall sideways and these in turn cause other pins to spin. Additional pin action results from the spinning.

Another factor related to the speed of the ball is the mechanics of ball action. A study done by the American Bowling Congress reveals the following data: When a ball leaves your hand, it does three things as it travels down the lane. It skids—slides forward without spinning or rotating; rolls—rotates forward in the direction of the pins; and takes—spins in such a way to cause the ball to hook, backup, or continue in a straight line (see table 1).

TABLE 1

MECHANICS OF BALL ACTION

	Normal speed (feet)	Too fast (feet)	Too slow (feet)
Skids	15	30	5
Rolls	25	25	25
Takes	20	5	30
Total	60	60	60

A normal ball has 20 feet of take, and a slow ball, 30 feet of take. That is why a slow ball fades and dies, causing 8–10, 5-pin, and other leaves. The ball dies or loses its spin before it reaches the pins.

The fast ball has a skid of 30 feet. Its roll is the same as the others at 25 feet, but it has only 5 feet of take. If you throw a hook ball and throw with too much speed, your ball will lose some of its sideward spin and so some of its action.

Here are ways to change the speed of your ball.

To Increase Speed

1. Hold the ball higher in address position.
2. Increase the length of your pushaway (the extention of your arms as you push the ball out from your body when taking your first step).
3. Speed up your approach.
4. Lengthen your approach.

To Decrease Speed

1. Hold ball lower in address position.
2. Shorten your pushaway.
3. Slow your approach.
4. Shorten your approach.

The weight of your ball is related to pin deflection. If your ball is too light, it will be deflected so much that pin action will be reduced. This is especially true if your ball also lacks sufficient velocity. Women sometimes have the problem of using a light ball and then lacking the strength to develop adequate speed. The combination of these two factors may cause a good pocket hit to take down only seven or eight pins. Using a slightly heavier ball or increasing the ball velocity by means of the suggestions above will correct this problem.

A good principle for both men and women is to use the heaviest ball you can control and yet still develop moderate speed. Swing the ball back and forth in a trial swing without dropping your shoulder, to tell if you can handle the ball without losing control.

SPOT VERSUS PIN BOWLING

There are advocates of both spot and pin methods of bowling, but most top flight bowlers use the spot-bowling technique. The essential difference is really quite simple: in pin bowling, your point of aim is the pins themselves; in spot bowling, the point of aim is either a dot or triangular-shaped "diamond" located a short distance from the foul line. There is a more detailed discussion of spot bowling in chapter 7.

LEARNING BOWLING THROUGH AUDIO-VISUAL CUES

What is the best way to learn how to roll a bowling ball properly? How do you do the pushaway, follow through correctly, hit the pocket, develop good form and obtain consistent results? And finally, how can you accomplish all the other essentials of good bowling technique?

The answer is *cues*—auditory and visual cues. Auditory cues are key words or catch phrases that present a concept. These cues include written words as well as the descriptions given by your instructor. With respect to the approach, for example, the phrase "perfect balance is essential to good bowling" is an auditory cue.

Visual cues, on the other hand, use checkpoints for ease in learning and remembering key movements or positions. A checkpoint or visual cue on the proper approach technique is the image of the ball being pushed away with your right arm fully extended as you take your first step. Visual cues refer to things that you can see for yourself.

These are just two illustrations of how audio-visual cues can be used. What follows is a discussion of how these techniques can help you learn the fundamental skills of the game. (Note that some cues must be reversed to apply to left-handers.) I have included several basic aspects of bowling: starting position, approach, and release of the ball. Let's look at them.

STARTING POSITION

Auditory Cues

1. Hold your body erect.
2. Shift your weight to your left foot.
3. Maintain a relaxed position.
4. To find your starting position, walk four and one-half steps back from the foul line.
5. Flex your knees slightly and shift your weight onto the balls of your feet.

Visual Cues or Checkpoints

1. Keep your feet far enough apart to maintain good balance and point your toes straight ahead.
2. Keep your right foot back of the left foot so that your right toe is opposite the midpoint of your left foot.
3. Hold the ball in a waist-high position in line with your right hip. (See figure 4.)
4. The palm of your right hand should face your chest with your thumb in the twelve-o'clock position to roll a straight ball. If you roll a hook, your palm should face to the left with your thumb in the ten o'clock-position. (See figures 5 and 6.)
5. Place your left hand beneath the ball on the left

Hold the ball in a waist-high
position in line with right hip.

FIGURE 4

To roll a straight ball, hold
your palm toward your chest
with your thumb in the twelve-
o'clock position.

FIGURE 5

To roll a hook, hold your palm
toward the left with your
thumb in the ten-o'clock
position.

FIGURE 6

side for support. Your little fingers should be touching each other.

6. With your right hand and wrist, form a straight line with your forearm.

7. Keep your right elbow snugly against your body.

APPROACH

Auditory Cues

1. Perfect balance is essential to good bowling.
2. Walk straight toward the target.
3. Don't rush your delivery.
4. Try to develop a smooth approach and release.
5. Use shuffle steps as in ballroom dancing.
6. A medium-fast ball is more effective than one "thrown through the back of the building."

Visual Cues or Checkpoints

1. Your first step should be a short one taken with your right foot (see figure 7).
2. As you take your first step, the ball should be pushed away and both arms fully extended (see figure 7).
3. Your left arm should assist your right in the pushaway.
4. As you complete the pushaway, drop your left hand off the ball and move your arm to the side to counterbalance the weight of the ball. Allow the ball to swing downward in a pendulum motion (see figures 8 and 9).
5. The pendulum swing should continue until the ball has swung back past your body to a waist-high position (see figure 10).

6. The remainder of the steps—four in all—should be done without specific concern for the position of the ball. The pendulum movement should be done without tightness or tension (see figures 11 and 12).
7. Your final step with your left foot, a sliding motion forward, should take place as you complete the forward swing of the ball (see figure 13).
8. Keep a firm wrist throughout the swing.

RELEASE OF THE BALL

Auditory Cues

1. Deliver the ball with smoothness and accuracy.
2. Correct follow-through is a key to consistent good bowling.
3. Good balance, important throughout the approach, is the essence of an accurate delivery.

Visual Cues or Checkpoints

1. On your final or fourth step, place your left foot next to your right and slide it straight forward.
2. Flex your left knee at a 90-degree angle as you complete the slide forward.
3. Point both feet straight down the alley.
4. Keep your body erect from the waist up.
5. Keep your shoulders square to the foul line.
6. Release the ball at a point in front of your left foot and in line with your right shoulder.
7. At the moment of release, keep your wrist straight and your thumb in the correct position (see figure 13).
8. In the follow-through, point your hand straight down the alley.

Your first step should be a short one taken with your right foot. As you step, push the ball away and fully extend both arms.

FIGURE 7

As you complete the pushaway, drop your left hand off the ball. Allow the ball to swing down in a pendulum motion while you take the second step.

FIGURE 8

The final part of the four-step delivery should be done without specific concern for the position of the ball.

FIGURE 11

Swing the ball forward without tightness or tension.

FIGURE 12

Continue the pendulum motion as you start to take the third step.

FIGURE 9

Let the ball swing back past your body to a waist-high position.

FIGURE 10

Your final step is a slide. At the moment of release, keep your wrist straight and your thumb in position.

FIGURE 13

As you release the ball, pull your hand up to ear height to obtain more spin on your ball.

FIGURE 14

9. As you release the ball, pull your hand up to shoulder height to obtain more spin on your ball (see figure 14).

10. To ensure proper balance, maintain the follow-through position for several seconds.

11. Watch your ball to see if it rolls over the proper spot or diamond.

IMPROVING YOUR SCORE THROUGH SPOT BOWLING

Do you need to be convinced that spot bowling is better than pin bowling? If so, consider these facts: (1) nine out of ten professionals use the spot-bowling method; (2) your concentration is more effective at 15 feet than at 60 to 65 feet; (3) you have less peripheral vision with a closer target and are therefore less affected by distractions in the immediate vicinity; and (4) a pin bowler is a spot bowler who does not look at the spot—a pin bowler must, however, roll over a spot to hit the target. Convinced? You probably will be as you master the technique. Here are the principles you need to understand and master.

ROLLING FOR STRIKES

Let's start out by helping you roll a strike ball using this technique (see figure 15). On the approach area you will notice three rows of dots that run parallel to the foul line. You will also notice some dark-colored, triangular-shaped pieces of wood, called diamonds, on the lane itself. A point between the 1 and 3 pins (or the 1–3 pocket) is our target for a strike ball. We

37

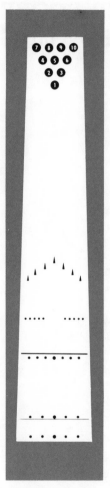

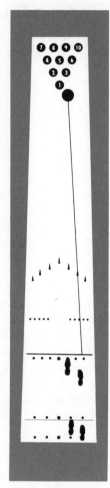

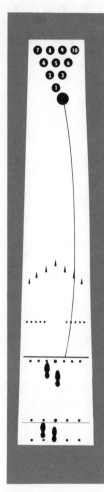

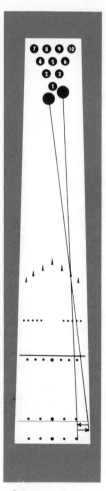

The second dia-
mond from the
right is the
target spot.

Straight-ball
bowlers make a
delivery from the
right side.

Hook-ball bowl-
ers move the start-
ing position to the
left.

Adjust to find
your exact start-
ing position.

FIGURE 15

SPOT BOWLING FOR STRIKES

are concerned with lining up three things: a starting position on the approach area, one of the diamonds on the lane, and the 1–3 pocket. We can definitely establish two of these right away. The second diamond from the right will be the "spot" on the lane and, of course, we want the ball to hit the 1–3 pocket. Now we need to determine the exact place for you to stand in order to roll the ball over that spot and into the strike zone. You can start out by assuming an approximate position and then adjusting yourself to discover the precise place. If you are a straight-ball bowler, you should start by placing your right foot on a board that is in line with the dot on the right side of the approach area (see figures 15 and 16). Your actual distance from the foul line will vary according to the length of your steps. If you roll a hook, you will need to move left of the dot two or more boards (see figure 15).

Now, you should sight down the lane and form an imaginary line from your position through the second diamond and into the 1–3 pocket. When you are ready to bowl, concentrate on the second diamond from the right, not on the pins. As you release the ball, try to roll it right over that second diamond. If you succeed in rolling the ball over the diamond and into the pocket for a good hit, the place you started from is the correct one for you. If, however, your ball did roll over the diamond but missed the pocket, you will need to adjust your starting position. The last illustration of figure 15 shows how the second diamond acts as a pivot point. Therefore, if you have missed the pocket on the right side, you move one board to your right from your original starting position. If you have missed the pocket on the left, you should move left one board. By doing this, you can determine your exact starting place. If you are

FIGURE 16
FOOT POSITION FOR STRIKE BALL

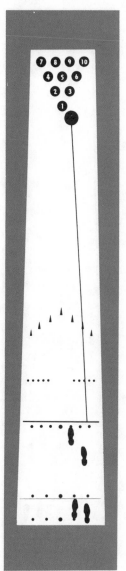

having any difficulty ask your instructor for help.

The key to spot bowling is consistency. To be successful, you must be able to roll the ball over a precise spot, and this is not easy at first. But your score and confidence will both go up once you achieve this valuable skill.

PICKING UP SPARES

Using the basic strike position, it is an easy matter to pick up certain middle spares with the straight ball. You can pick up the 5 pin, the 5–8 spare, the 1–2–5 spare, and the 1–2–9 spare merely by rolling the strike ball (see figure 17).

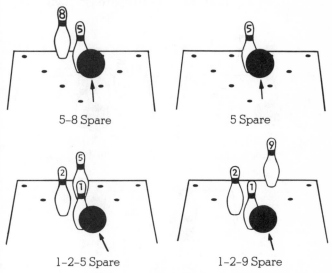

5–8 Spare   5 Spare

1–2–5 Spare   1–2–9 Spare

These middle spares can be picked up by using the strike ball

FIGURE 17

The 8 pin can be hit easily by moving one board right of your usual strike position on the approach area. By moving one board left of your strike position, the 9 pin can be picked up.

The 1–2–4–7 leave, or "fence," the 2 pin, and the 2–8 spare can be picked up by moving two boards to the right of your strike position (see figure 18). Remember that in all of these middle spares, the spot to aim for is the second diamond from the right.

Next, let's look at the perimeter spares. These include the 7 pin, the 4 pin, the 4–7 spare, the 4–7–8 spare, the 2–7 split, the 7–8 spare, and the 2–4–7 spare on the left of the lane (see figure 19). On the other side of the lane we can pick up the 10 pin, the 6 pin, the 6–10 spare, the 6–9–10 spare, the 3–10 split, the 9–10 spare, and the 3–6–10 spare (see figure 20).

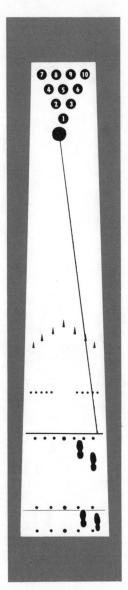

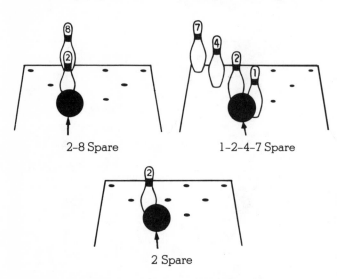

2–8 Spare   1–2–4–7 Spare

2 Spare

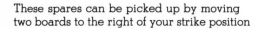

These spares can be picked up by moving two boards to the right of your strike position

FIGURE 18

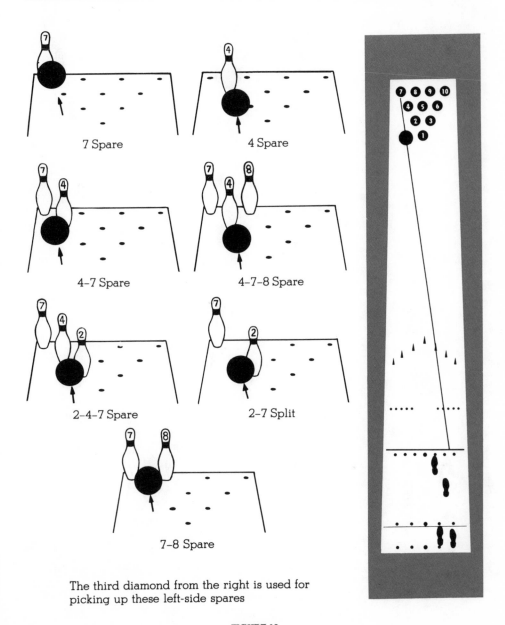

7 Spare

4 Spare

4–7 Spare

4–7–8 Spare

2–4–7 Spare

2–7 Split

7–8 Spare

The third diamond from the right is used for picking up these left-side spares

FIGURE 19

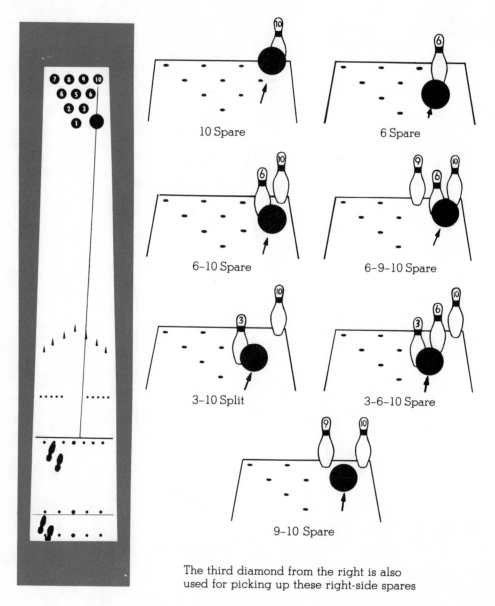

10 Spare

6 Spare

6–10 Spare

6–9–10 Spare

3–10 Split

3–6–10 Spare

9–10 Spare

The third diamond from the right is also used for picking up these right-side spares

FIGURE 20

Let's examine the 7-pin pickup first. Instead of taking your usual strike position, place your right foot on the outermost board of the lane proper. This is the black line in figure 21. Now move four boards left of this position. This is an approximate starting place for a straight-ball bowler. (If your lane has seven dots in the approach area rather than five, as shown in figure 21, your right foot will be on the first dot in from the right side of the lane.)

Hook bowlers will have to move farther to the left. Your spot (both hook and straight bowlers) for this pickup and all other perimeter spares is the third diamond from the right side of the alley. As you prepare to roll the ball, your feet should be pointed toward the third diamond and in line with the 7 pin. If your ball goes over the diamond but misses the pin, you need to adjust as you did for the strike ball. A miss on the right side of the pin calls for a move one board to the right. And a miss on the left side indicates a move of one board to the left. Thus you always move in the direction your ball was off.

A move of one board left from your 7-pin pickup position will enable you to pick up the 4 pin, the 4–7, the 4–7–8, the 2–4–7, and the 7–8 spares as well as the 2–7 split (see figure 21).

For the 10-pin pickup move to the left side of the approach area and place your left foot on the last board of the lane. Hook-ball bowlers can roll from this position, but if you roll a straight ball, move four boards to the right (see figure 22). Again sight over the same third diamond from the right, point your toes in that direction, and roll the ball. If you hit the diamond but miss the pin, make the necessary adjustment to determine your correct 10-pin position.

The 6 pin, the 6–10, the 6–9–10, the 3–6–10, and the 9–10 spares as well as the 3–10 split are picked up

FIGURE 21

FOOT POSITION FOR 7-PIN SPARE

FIGURE 22

FOOT POSITION FOR 10-PIN SPARE

by moving one board right from your 10-pin position (see figure 22).

These are not the only spares that can be picked up using spot bowling, but they are a good start. The five most frequent spares—as determined in a study conducted by the American Machine & Foundry Company—are all covered here. They are, in order of frequency, the 10, the 7, the 5, the 1-2-4, and the 6-10. By the time you have mastered the spares shown, you will probably be able to figure out other possibilities for yourself. For your convenience, a quick reference sheet for spot bowling follows. A tear-out version of the same sheet appears on page 87 of this book; a version for left-handers is on page 89.

QUICK REFERENCE SHEET
FOR SPOT BOWLING

Strike Ball, 5-8 Spare, 1-2-5 Spare, 1-2-9 Spare

1. Place your right foot on the dot at the right side of the approach area.
2. Point toes toward 1-3 pocket.
3. Roll ball over the second diamond from the right side of the lane. If you roll a hook, your starting position will be three or four boards to the left of the first dot.

Five Pin

1. Line up for strike ball.
2. Roll ball over second diamond from the right. Hook-ball bowlers will have to move left one board from the strike position.

Two Pin, 1-2-4-7 Spare, 2-8 Spare

1. Move two boards to the right of your strike position.

2. Roll ball over the second diamond from the right into 1–2 pocket.

Ten Pin

1. Place left foot on last board on the left side of the lane.
2. Move four boards to your right.
3. Point toes toward 10 pin.
4. Roll ball over third diamond from the right side of the lane. If you roll a hook, start from the last board on the left side of the lane.

Six Pin, 6-10 Spare, 6-9-10 Spare, 3-6-10 Spare, 9-10 Spare, 3-10 Split

1. Move right one board from your position for the 10-pin pickup.
2. Roll ball over third diamond from the right side of the lane.

Seven Pin

1. Place your right foot on the last board on the right side of the lane.
2. Move four boards to your left.
3. Point your toes at the 7 pin.
4. Roll ball over third diamond from the right side of the lane. If you roll a hook, start eight boards from the right side of the lane.

Four Pin, 4-7 Spare, 4-7-8 Spare, 2-4-7 Spare, 7-8 Spare, 2-7 Split

1. Move left one board from your position for the 7-pin pickup.
2. Roll ball over third diamond from the right side of the lane.

TABLE 2

SPOT BOWLING CHECKSHEET

Strike ball target: Second diamond from the right, right-handers.
Second diamond from the left, left-handers.

10 and 7 pin pickup target: Third diamond from the right, right-handers.
Third diamond from the left, left-handers.

As you roll each frame, put an X to indicate where your ball rolled in relation to the targeted diamond.

Example: △x △x

Strike ball	*10 Pin*	*7 Pin*
1. △	1. △	1. △
2. △	2. △	2. △
3. △	3. △	3. △
4. △	4. △	4. △
5. △	5. △	5. △
6. △	6. △	6. △
7. △	7. △	7. △
8. △	8. △	8. △
9. △	9. △	9. △
10. △	10. △	10. △

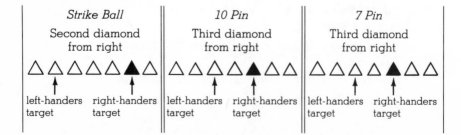

Strike Ball	*10 Pin*	*7 Pin*
Second diamond from right	Third diamond from right	Third diamond from right
left-handers target / right-handers target	left-handers target / right-handers target	left-handers target / right-handers target

SPOT BOWLING CHECKSHEET

The spot bowling checksheet (table 2) is designed to be used when you are practicing spare pickups or when you are actually rolling a game. The checksheet will help you become more consistent in hitting the spots.

8

HOW TO KEEP SCORE

Scoring in bowling can appear quite complicated until you catch on to it. It will be helpful if you can keep these things in mind:

1. A game consists of ten frames, represented by the ten boxes on the scoresheet. You roll two balls in each frame unless you roll a strike with your first ball.

2. When you roll a strike, you get a score of 10 plus the number of pins toppled on the next two balls. You do not record your score for the strike frame until you have rolled the next two balls.

3. A spare is scored when you knock down all ten pins with two rolls. Your score for that frame is 10 plus the number of pins you knock down with the first ball in the next frame. You do not record your score for the frame in which you have made a spare until you have rolled your first ball in the next frame.

4. There is a system of symbols you must learn in scoring. These symbols help you to keep track

of what is happening as you roll your game. They are also helpful in analyzing the strengths and weaknesses of your game.

The symbols used in scoring are presented here and are followed by a sample game.

SYMBOLS USED IN SCORING

Spare All pins are knocked down with two balls in a frame.

Strike All ten pins are knocked down with the first ball in a frame.

Miss (Error or Blow) Failure to bowl down all ten pins with two balls in a frame, except in the case of a split.

Split (Railroad) A leave in which the head pin is down and two or more pins remain standing with adjacent pins knocked down in front and between.

Converted Split A split which becomes a spare when the pins are picked up with the second ball in a frame.

Some situations can arise that may make scoring a bit more difficult:

Foul on First Ball The bowler gets no score for the first ball and pins must be reracked for the second ball.

Foul on Second Ball No score is recorded for the second ball, so the total for the frame is the first ball count only.

Recording Both Balls on Scoresheet In our scoring sample (see below), only the score of the first ball is specially marked, though the score of the second ball may be calculated from this figure and the total. The method used in the example and the one that shows the score of both balls are shown here.

Strike Followed by Spare Score 20 for the strike frame since a strike gives 10 points plus the total of the next two balls.

Spare Followed by Strike Score 20 for the spare frame since a spare gives 10 points plus the score of the next ball.

Double When you roll two strikes in succession, you must wait until you roll a third ball before posting a score in the first frame.

Turkey or Triple When you roll three strikes in succession, score 30 for the first strike frame.

Strike Out A strike in the tenth frame followed by strikes with both bonus balls gives 30 points the final frame.

8	9	10
8 –	5 –	X X X
130	135	165

Strike in the Tenth Frame Roll two extra balls to determine your score for the final frame.

8	9	10
8 −	X	X 6 3
130	156	175

Spare in the Tenth Frame Roll one extra ball to determine your score for the final frame.

8	9	10
8 −	7 −	9 ╱ 7
130	137	154

SCORING A SAMPLE GAME

First Frame You roll two balls and knock down a total of seven pins, so you mark that number in the first frame and a (−) in the box to indicate the miss or error.

1	2	3	4	5	6	7	8	9	10
7 −									
7									

Second Frame On your first ball, you knock down all but the 7 and 10 pins. Circle the 8 to show the split. With your second ball you take out the 7 pin, giving you nine for the frame and a total of 16 for the first two frames. Put 1 in the box to show you knocked down the 7 pin.

1	2	3	4	5	6	7	8	9	10
7 −	⑧ 1								
7	16								

Third Frame This time you make your spare. Your first ball leaves only the 5 pin, and you knock it down with the second ball. Put a (/) in the box, but do not mark any score for the third frame. Having spared, your first ball's total in the next frame will be added to your score for the first three frames.

1	2	3	4	5	6	7	8	9	10
7 –	⑧ /	9 /							
7	16								

Fourth Frame You knock down seven pins with your first ball. Add 17 to your second frame (10 for the spare plus 7 for the first ball in this frame). Your second ball knocks down two more pins but leaves one standing, so add 9 to your score and put a 2 in the box.

1	2	3	4	5	6	7	8	9	10
7 –	⑧ /	9 /	7 2						
7	16	33	42						

Fifth Frame Here, you register your first strike. Put the (X) in the box and wait for the next two rolls before you compute your score.

1	2	3	4	5	6	7	8	9	10
7 –	⑧ /	9 /	7 2	✗					
7	16	33	42						

Sixth Frame   Your first ball leaves a 3–10 split. Circle 8 to show the split. Your second ball converts the split to a spare. Draw a (/) in the box to indicate this conversion. Add 20 to your fourth frame total (10 plus 8 plus 2) for your fifth frame total. Wait for your first ball in the seventh frame before computing your sixth frame total.

1	2	3	4	5	6	7	8	9	10
7 –	⑧ /	9 /	7 2	☒	⑧ /				
7	16	33	42	62					

Seventh Frame   You score your second strike of the game. You put an (X) in the box and wait for your next two balls before figuring your total for this frame. Your sixth frame can now be recorded. Add 20 (10 plus 10) to your fifth frame total.

1	2	3	4	5	6	7	8	9	10
7 –	⑧ /	9 /	7 2	☒	⑧ /	☒			
7	16	33	42	62	82				

Eighth Frame   On your first ball you take down nine pins but fail to convert with the second ball. Put a (–) in the box to record the miss. Add 19 (10 plus 9) to the sixth frame total to get your seventh frame score. The nine pins are then added to the seventh frame total to complete scoring in the eighth frame.

1	2	3	4	5	6	7	8	9	10
7 –	⑧ /	9 /	7 2	☒	⑧ /	☒	9 –		
7	16	33	42	62	82	101	110		

Ninth Frame You strike again! This means you put an (X) in the box and wait till you roll your next two balls before you figure your ninth frame total.

1	2	3	4	5	6	7	8	9	10
7 –	⑧ 1	9 /	7 2	X	⑧ /	X	9 –	X	
7	16	33	42	62	82	101	110		

Tenth Frame Your ball goes right in the pocket and you roll another strike. That gives you two more rolls. With the first of the next two rolls, you knock down eight pins. This adds 28 to your eighth frame total (10 plus 10 plus 8). With your next and final ball, you pick up the remaining two pins. This means you add 20 (10 plus 8 plus 2) for the tenth frame. Your total score for the game is 158.

1	2	3	4	5	6	7	8	9	10
7 –	⑧ 1	9 /	7 2	X	⑧ /	X	9 –	X	X 8 /
7	16	33	42	62	82	101	110	138	158

BOWLING RULES:
A SYNOPSIS

Official bowling competition in the United States is conducted under the auspices of the ABC and the WIBC. For all of its league and tournament competition, the WIBC adopted the ABC rules. The following summarizes the most significant official rules and regulations as established by the ABC.

1. The overall length of a bowling lane shall be 62 feet, 10 and $^3/_{16}$ inches from foul line to pit edge. It must be 60 feet from the foul line to the center of the 1-pin spot. The width of the lane must not exceed 42 inches nor be less than 41 inches. A diagram of a lane is shown in figure 23.

2. Approved pins shall be made of sound, hard maple. Pins constructed of material other than wood, such as synthetic material or plastic-coated wood, may be used but must comply with ABC specifications. The weight of the standard wood pin must not exceed 3 pounds, 10 ounces or be less than 3 pounds, 2 ounces. The height of pins must be 15 inches.

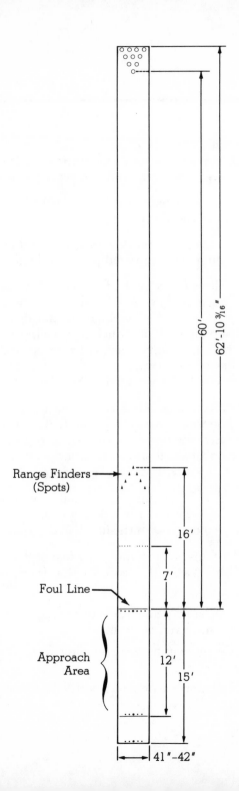

Range Finders
(Spots)

60'

62'-10 ³/₁₆ "

16'

7'

Foul Line

Approach
Area

12'

15'

41"-42"

FIGURE 23

DIMENSIONS OF A LANE

3. Bowling balls shall not exceed 27 inches in circumference. Figure 24 shows a pin and ball. The ball must weigh no more than 16 pounds.

4. Pins that are knocked down by a ball that first entered the gutter do not count.

5. Pins that bounce off the lane, rebound, and remain standing are considered pins standing.

6. If the bowler or any part of his or her body touches or goes beyond the foul line and touches any part of the bowling lane during or after delivery, it is a foul. Touching a wall, post, division board, or any other structure beyond the foul line constitutes a foul. Walls adjacent to end lanes should have a vertical foul line.

7. A foul ball counts as a ball rolled, but the pins that are knocked down do not count. After the pins are reset, the bowler is allowed to roll her or his second ball. If she or he knocks all the pins down, a spare, not a strike is given.

8. If a bowler fouls on the second ball, the pins knocked down with that ball do not count. The pins knocked down with the first ball do count.

9. If a bowler fouls on both his or her first and second ball in a frame, the score for that frame is zero.

10. A ball is declared "dead," the pins are reset, and the bowler must roll again if:

    a. One or more pins were missing from the setup.

    b. The ball comes in contact with any foreign object.

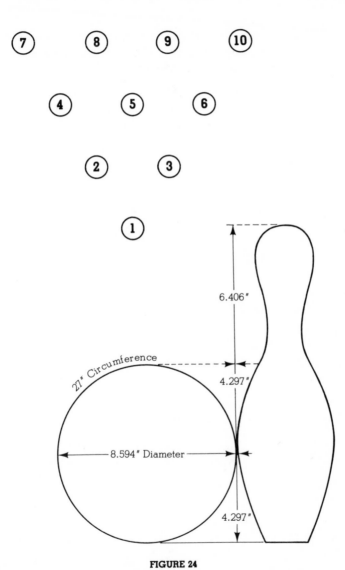

FIGURE 24

POSITION OF PINS
AND SIZE OF PIN AND BALL

c. A human pinsetter removes or interferes with any pin before the ball stops rolling or before it reaches the pins.

d. A bowler is interfered with while making his delivery, providing he calls attention to this fact before the ball reaches the pins.

10

BOWLING
IN COMPETITION

No matter how casual your interest in bowling may be when your first learn the game, the challenge of bettering your previous efforts will grow. As your skill improves, you are likely to develop a real zest for competition. Many bowlers find the excitement of competing against others the most satisfying experience of the sport.

HANDICAP LEAGUES

For regular bowling competition, most people join a group at their local bowling establishment and bowl on a five-person team in an organized league. The use of handicaps enables bowlers of different abilities to roll in the same league. There are various ways of computing handicaps, and two systems are presented here. The first one is for beginning bowlers (table 3); the second is for intermediate or advanced bowlers. In either case, a bowler with a 180 average is referred to as a scratch bowler, or a bowler who does not have any handicap.

TABLE 3

HANDICAPS FOR BEGINNERS

A H	A H	A H	A H	A H	A H
60–108	80–90	100–72	120–54	140–36	160–18
61–107	81–89	101–71	121–53	141–35	161–17
62–106	82–88	102–70	122–52	142–34	162–16
63–105	83–87	103–69	123–51	143–33	163–15
64–104	84–86	104–68	124–50	144–32	164–14
65–103	85–85	105–67	125–49	145–31	165–13
66–102	86–84	106–66	126–48	146–30	166–12
67–101	87–83	107–65	127–47	147–29	167–11
68–100	88–82	108–64	128–46	148–28	168–10
69–99	89–81	109–63	129–45	149–27	169–9
70–99	90–81	110–63	130–45	150–27	170–9
71–98	91–80	111–62	131–44	151–26	171–8
72–97	92–79	112–61	132–43	152–25	172–7
73–96	93–78	113–60	133–42	153–24	173–6
74–95	94–77	114–59	134–41	154–23	174–5
75–94	95–76	115–58	135–40	155–22	175–4
76–93	96–75	116–57	136–39	156–21	176–3
77–92	97–74	117–56	137–38	157–20	177–2
78–91	98–73	118–55	138–37	158–19	178–1
79–90	99–72	119–54	139–36	159–18	179–0
					180–0

Note: The table gives the corresponding handicap (H) for a person's average (A) between 60 and 180. The handicap represents 90 percent of the difference between each average and 180. Any person with an average of 180 or over receives no handicap.

TABLE 4
HANDICAPS FOR INTERMEDIATE
AND ADVANCED BOWLERS

A H	A H	A H	A H	A H	A H
55–94	76–78	97–62	118–47	139–31	160–15
56–93	77–77	98–62	119–46	140–30	161–14
57–92	78–77	99–61	120–45	141–29	162–14
58–92	79–76	100–60	121–44	142–29	163–13
59–91	80–75	101–59	122–44	143–28	164–12
60–90	81–74	102–59	123–43	144–27	165–11
61–89	82–74	103–58	124–42	145–26	166–11
62–89	83–73	104–57	125–41	146–26	167–10
63–88	84–72	105–56	126–41	147–25	168–9
64–87	85–71	106–56	127–40	148–24	169–8
65–86	86–71	107–55	128–39	149–23	170–8
66–86	87–70	108–54	129–38	150–23	171–7
67–85	88–69	109–53	130–38	151–22	172–6
68–84	89–68	110–53	131–37	152–21	173–5
69–83	90–68	111–52	132–36	153–20	174–5
70–83	91–67	112–51	133–35	154–20	175–4
71–82	92–66	113–50	134–35	155–19	176–3
72–81	93–65	114–50	135–34	156–18	177–2
73–80	94–65	115–49	136–33	157–17	178–2
74–80	95–64	116–48	137–32	158–17	179–1
75–79	96–63	117–47	138–32	159–16	180–0

Note: The table gives the handicap (H) for any person's average (A) between 55 and 180. The handicap represents 75 percent of the difference between each average and 180; a person with an average of 180 or more receives no handicap.

LEAGUE COMPETITION

Figure 25 provides a scoresheet for a typical handicap league. Note how Hearn, leadoff person of the Hilltoppers, is a key in the Hilltoppers' victory. Going

TEAMS _HILLTOPPERS_ VS _WHIRLWINDS_

PLAYER	HDCP	1	2	3	4	5	6	7	8	9	10	TOTAL
1 HEARN	57	9	17	37	55	63	72	91	110	128	137	137
2 GOLDMAN	43	9	18	27	46	65	74	94	109	126	135	135
3 GOSS	0	20	40	57	77	97	117	137	151	171	201	201
4 GOLDBERG	0	9	29	47	56	73	82	91	100	109	137	137
5 TOTAL	100											610 +100
6												710

MARKS	Hilltoppers	1/	3/	6/	9/	12/	13/	16/	19/	22/	28/	
	Whirlwinds ⑤	6/	10/	12/	13/	14/	17/	19/	20/	21/	24/	
8 JOSEFSON	57	8	25	41	49	57	75	83	92	101	120	120
9 KELLAN	45	9	25	31	40	49	68	77	86	112	132	132
10 LANG	41	1	21	41	54	61	69	82	90	99	105	105
11 JUMP	7	20	37	46	55	74	94	114	133	142	160	160
12 TOTAL	150											517 +150 667

FIGURE 25

SAMPLE SCORESHEET FOR A HANDICAP LEAGUE

into the game he or she carried a 104 average which rated a handicap of 57. The 137 game coupled with the handicap of 57 gave Hearn a total of 194. This was good enough to beat Jump, the best bowler on the Whirlwinds. Jump, the opponent's anchor person, carried a 171 average and a handicap of seven. She or he rolled a very respectable 160 but a handicap of seven, added to her or his score, gave a total of 167, 27 pins less than Hearn's total. This illustrates how the handicap system enables all bowlers to compete on an equal basis regardless of the difference in their abilities.

A running account of the match, from frame to frame, was kept by totaling cumulative marks (strikes or spares) as the game progressed (see the numbers divided by diagonal lines at the center of the scoresheet). This is an unofficial way to keep track of how one team is doing in competition with another. It is an approximate measure, but it makes the game more exciting because you don't have to wait til the end to see who is winning. At the beginning of the game each team captain adds up the handicaps for his or her team. The Hilltoppers had a total of 100, while the Whirlwinds had a team handicap of 150. Since each bowler's handicap is determined by his or her current average, the team with the smaller handicap, the Hilltoppers, would be the better overall bowlers. However, the Hilltoppers *have* to bowl better than the Whirlwinds to win because of the fifty-pin difference in the two teams' handicaps. To indicate this difference at the start of the game, the Whirlwinds were given 5 marks (indicated by the number in the circle). Each mark represents ten pins, and thus the 5 marks represent the fifty-pin difference in team handicaps.

The Hilltoppers did not overtake their opponents until the ninth frame. A triple (three strikes consecutively) by Goss in the last frame really helped provide the margin of victory.

TOURNAMENTS

For those who seek more difficult tests of their bowling skills, there are numerous bowling tournaments conducted at the state, regional, and national levels. The most prominent tournaments are the annual ABC and WIBC championships.

The ABC championship is conducted in the following categories:

1. Classic Division, for professional bowlers who average 190 or more.

2. Regular Division, for outstanding bowlers who are not professionals.

3. Booster Division, for five-man teams whose members average 170 or less.

In the Classic and Regular Divisions, competition is conducted for five-man teams, doubles (two-man teams), singles (individual bowlers), and all events. All events contenders must participate in team, doubles, and singles competition.

The WIBC championships are held in the following categories:

1. Open Division, for bowlers with averages of 171 and over.

2. Division I, for bowlers with averages of 146 through 170.

3. Division II, for bowlers with averages of 145 and under.

Competition is held for teams, doubles, singles, and all events.

As college students you will be interested in the intercollegiate bowling championship conducted by the Association of College Unions. These tournaments have been made possible through financial grants provided by the American Machine & Foundry Company and the Brunswick Corporation with the cooperation of the ABC. Started in 1954, this intercollegiate competition was initially conducted by a comparison of scores submitted by mail. In 1959 the first National Face-to-Face Men's Intercollegiate Bowling Tournament was held. Through the cooperation of the WIBC, a similar tournament for college women was held in 1962 for the first time. During the summer of 1966 representatives of all the major organized bowling groups met and helped form a new Collegiate Division. The following information is taken from official data concerning this organization.

The Collegiate Division

The establishment of the Collegiate Division by both the ABC and the WIBC stems directly from their years of active cooperation with the Association of College Unions-International (ACU-I) in conducting annual intercollegiate bowling championships. After a prolonged and detailed analysis of collegiate bowling, these organizations concluded that a nationally sanctioned program designed to provide service and assistance to the college community and college participants would also serve the better interests of bowling in general.

Participation in the ACU-I Bowling Tournament is dependent upon payment of a Collegiate Division membership fee of 75¢ (in 1980) per person per year. Collegiate Division fees will pay for the services of the

ABC and WIBC. (In addition to this fee, Collegiate Division rules allow local collegiate organizations to assess a maximum fee of $1.25 per person per year to finance local activities. The total allowable fee in 1980 is $2.00.)

The key figure on each campus in the formation, structuring, and operation of the ACU-I Collegiate Division program is the campus representative elected, approved, or appointed by the local college or university authority responsible for the bowling program. This person, as the advisor, will simultaneously represent the local student organization, the ABC-WIBC, and the Recreation Committee of the ACU-I.

It is strongly recommended that all students participating in bowling activities sponsored or approved by the ACU-I or any college or university that belongs to the ACU-I be sanctioned by the Collegiate Division. Information about the Collegiate Division can be obtained by writing American Bowling Congress/Women's International Bowling Congress, Collegiate Division, 5301 South 76th Street, Greendale, Wisconsin 53129.

SPECIAL EVENTS

As a change of pace from the usual league-type bowling competition, there are a number of special events that can add fun to your bowling experience. They can be adapted to singles, doubles, team, mixed competition, or almost any combination of these, and endless variations can be made in the rules to suit your situation. Most of the events described here are included through the courtesy of the National Bowling Council (NBC), 1919 Pennsylvania Avenue N.W., Washington, D.C. 20006.

Beat the Champ (NBC)

Announce a beat-the-champ tournament. The champ can be the top intramural bowler of your college or the winner of an all-campus tournament. Ask the champ to roll a target score and then have those who entered the competition try to beat this score. The tournament can also start with the contestants rolling a single game or a three-game series; then the champ can roll his or her games.

Blind Bowling

Hang a wire with a curtain about halfway down the lane to block the bowler's view of the pins. With automatic pin machines showing the pins remaining, regular scoring can be used. This is excellent practice for spot bowling.

Best Ball (NBC)

A doubles team competition is just right for a best ball event. The partners bowl on adjacent lanes. The first player on each team rolls the first ball. If that player scores a strike, that team has a strike in the first frame. If that player fails to make a strike, his or her partner tries for the strike. If neither strikes, each tries to make a spare. The highest count of either team member is the team score for that frame.

Variations include two lower-average bowlers competing against a single higher-average bowler. Their two chances at a strike or spare provide the necessary handicap to make the match interesting.

Head Pin

Each bowler rolls only one ball per frame. The score for that frame is the number of pins knocked down, providing the head pin goes down. If the head pin is missed, the score for that frame is zero. Twelve balls are allowed, and a perfect game is twelve strikes or 120 points.

Free-Strike Tournaments (NBC)

Free-strike tournaments offer many variations. A free strike can be given in the first frame, or the first ball in the tenth frame is also a great free-strike spot. Another possibility is that a series of free strikes can be awarded for the strategic third, sixth, and ninth frames. Each bowler automatically receives these strikes in the predetermined frame or frames. They are recorded on the scoresheet, and then the bowlers roll their regular game. The games are over quickly, and the scores are really high—great confidence builders. It is not unusual for bowlers to conveniently avoid mentioning the free strikes when they report their scores to friends.

Golf Bowling (NBC)

The low-score idea is used in this event. Each bowler rolls ten frames. A strike counts as one stroke, a spare counts as two, and if any pins are standing after the second ball, the bowlers receive a score of three. The lowest score possible is 10; the highest, 30.

Scotch Doubles (NBC)

In this type of doubles play one partner rolls the first ball, his or her partner rolls the second. The partners continue alternate rolling throughout the game.

Wild Strike (NBC)

In the wild-strike tournament each bowler rolls a single game in the usual fashion, but after the game is completed, he or she is allowed to replace any frame with a strike.

SPECIAL EVENTS FOR SPECIAL PEOPLE

Bowling is a sport in which a wide variety of people can participate. Young children, senior citizens, and the physically and mentally handicapped can all enjoy bowling.

As your skill and knowledge move up the scale, you may want to help some of these special people experience the fun of bowling. You could become a teacher-coach in an American Junior Bowling Congress league in your community. Bowling competition for handicapped children through the Special Olympics might be a program of interest to you. Or you might want to volunteer as a bowling instructor for a program offered by your local senior-citizens center. Some bowling establishments provide special railings that enable blind persons to bowl. You could become involved in a community project to help purchase such equipment.

Your bowling instructor can provide you with information about these programs. Get involved; you'll be glad you did.

11

TIPS FOR
ADVANCED BOWLERS

What really happens when a bowler makes a strike? Why is a hook ball considered better than a straight ball, and what is a full-roller? When you get curious about the answers to these questions, you are probably moving beyond the beginning stage and are getting ready for more advanced information and play. Keep in mind, however, that skilled performers in any sport keep working constantly to perfect the basic techniques. Smoothness, rhythm, balance, follow-through, and consistency will remain important skills for you to master completely.

But let's move ahead into what can make you a more accomplished bowler, now that you are acquainted with the basics.

THE HOOK BALL

Why is the hook ball more effective than the straight ball in producing strikes? The answer lies in the angle at which the hook ball contacts the 1 or head pin. Figure 26 shows a perfect strike in which the ball first goes into the 1–3 pocket. There it topples the 1 pin, which then knocks over the 2, 4, and 7 pins, in domino fashion. When the ball hits the 1 pin, the ball is deflected and hits the 3 pin. The 3 pin then pushes into the 6 pin, which takes out the 10 pin. The ball meanwhile continues on its way, knocking out the 5 and 9 pins. Then the 5 pin is pushed into the 8 pin by the ball's action, and you have made yourself a perfect strike. Note that there are four points at which the ball contacts pins—at the 1, 3, 5, and 9 pins. For a strike to happen, the ball has to hit the 1 pin exactly where it is on the centerline of the 1–2–4–7 line (see figure 26).

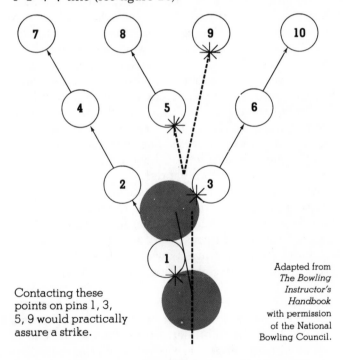

Contacting these points on pins 1, 3, 5, 9 would practically assure a strike.

Adapted from
*The Bowling
Instructor's
Handbook*
with permission
of the National
Bowling Council.

FIGURE 26
CONTACT POINTS FOR A PERFECT STRIKE

The hook ball, which curves to the left as it comes into the 1–3 pocket, approaches the 1 pin on the 1–2–4–7 centerline more directly head on than a straight ball does. This enhances the possibility of starting off the correct sequence of events that make for a strike.

Full-Roller, Semi-Roller, and Spinner

The average score for men who bowl in a league is 159; the average for women is 132. If your average is much below these figures, you probably need to continue practicing your basic skills, which includes learning how to throw a hook ball. As you begin to move above these averages, you can begin to examine the type of ball you are throwing. There are three basic types of hook balls: the full-roller, the semi-roller, and the spinner. All three are rolled with either the thumb at ten o'clock and ring finger at four o'clock or the thumb at eleven o'clock and ring finger at five o'clock. The difference between these three rolls occurs in the release. The next time you bowl, look at your ball after you have rolled a few times. The accumulation of oil and dust from the lanes will make a ring around your ball (see figure 27). You are most apt to see this ring between the thumbhole and the finger holes, circling the middle of the ball. This is a full-roller and is the easiest roll for the average or slightly above average bowler because the ball is released with a straight lifting action and little or no turn of the hand. (Some bowling experts, however, maintain that there is a slight turn of the thumbhole in a clockwise manner from ten towards eleven o'clock with the full-roller. This occurs as the ball is lifted with the fingers at the point of release.

The semiroller has the ring below the center of the ball. To do this, the wrist remains straight, and the thumb is turned in a counterclockwise direction from ten to nine o'clock as the ball is lifted with the fingers. This is a more difficult skill to master, but it does make the ball hook more sharply, and this drives it into the 1–2–4–7 pins at the best angle for a strike.

Full-Roller   Semiroller   Spinner

FIGURE 27

DUST LINES ON THE THREE TYPES OF ROLLS

The spinner has the ring even lower than the semiroller and is generally not recommended for most bowlers because it requires unusual wrist action. The counterclockwise turn of the hand at release is quite pronounced and requires a delicate touch to perfect.

VARIABLES THAT AFFECT THE HOOK

If your hook ball is to be effective and consistent, you should be aware of the variables that affect the amount your ball hooks.

Hand Position

If your thumb is at eleven o'clock and your ring finger is at four o'clock, your ball will have a slight hook. If your thumb is at ten o'clock and ring finger is at four o'clock, you will get more hooking action. The rotation of your hand in a counterclockwise manner, as in the semiroller, exaggerates the hook even more. Whatever hand position you use, be aware that your delivery may vary somewhat from day to day. Practice is important. It's what keeps this day-to-day variation to a minimum.

Ball Speed

By decreasing the speed of your ball, you can increase the amount of hook. To reduce the hook, increase the ball speed. Tips for changing the speed of your ball are listed on page 27.

Lane Conditions

The amount of dressing or lane oil on the lanes definitely affects the amount of hook. The more dressing, the less the ball will hook because of reduced friction. The oil causes your ball to skid more, and so rotation is reduced.

Ball Position at Release

If you release your ball right at the foul line rather than some distance beyond the foul line, your ball will have farther to travel to get to the pins, so your ball will begin to lose some rotation, which results in a lessened hook. That is why it is recommended that you release your ball 15–18 inches beyond the foul line for best hooking action. Remember, though, not to touch anything on the lane beyond the foul line.

Wrist Position

If your hand is bent slightly forward, rather than having your wrist straight at release, the hook will be exaggerated. A straight wrist helps you develop a consistent hook.

Lift

Lift is the upward pressure applied by the fingers to the ball at the moment of release. The more lift you apply, the more your ball hooks. To be most effective, the lift should be applied by the fingers as your thumb begins to clear the thumb hole. The force for the lift is increased if you bend your arm upward at the elbow at the moment of release. If you follow through until your thumb reaches shoulder height you will insure the proper elbow bend.

Grip

You can roll a hook with the conventional grip, but the semifingertip and fingertip ball increase the hooking action (see page 84 and figure 28).

You have control over all the variables listed above except the lane conditions. When you change any one variable, however, it is important to keep everything else constant. Some changes will work well for some bowlers, and others will not. Ask your instructor to help you find which variables work best for you. Consistency and ample rotation as your ball reaches the pocket are your goals.

Here is a final and important note for adjusting your hook ball for both strikes and spares. If on a given day you find your ball is hooking more than usual or less than usual as you roll your pregame warmup balls, don't make any big changes in your technique. Change your starting position instead. Move left perhaps one board if your ball is hooking more than usual or move one board right if your ball is hooking less than usual. This is assuming that you are using a precise aiming point as advocated in the spot-bowling section of this book. Keep the same aiming point, but change your starting position to make the necessary adjustment. Remember, this holds true for *both* your strike ball and your spare pickups.

If you want to make a change in the type of hook ball you roll using one of the variables mentioned here, firmly establish the new technique through practice. Don't attempt to do it while bowling in competition. Practice does indeed make perfect.

EXERCISES TO IMPROVE YOUR HOOK BALL

If, with the help of your instructor, you decide to try mastering the full-roller or semiroller, you will need to snap your two middle fingers to your palm as you release the ball. This action increases the spin or rotation on the ball. Considerable strength in your middle fingers is required to do this forcefully, and one way to develop this is to practice lifting your ball from the floor, using only your two middle fingers. Start by lifting the ball five times and build up to thirty lifts. Next, practice rolling the ball on the lanes but hold the ball with just your two middle fingers. To do this, stand just back of the foul line, bend your knees, pick up the ball with two fingers, and swing it back and forth in a pendulum motion, just a few inches off the lane. After a couple of swings, roll the ball down the lane. You will be amazed how much your strength and control increase with this exercise program.

Your index and little fingers also play an important part in making an effective delivery. Remember, a straight wrist is necessary when releasing the ball in order to roll a hook that has good action. Your forefinger and little finger can maintain that straight-wrist position. If you press against the ball with these fingers just before you start your pushaway and maintain that pressure throughout your delivery, you will find that your wrist remains straight.

Weighting the Ball

Earlier reference has been made about the effect the overall weight of your ball has on your ability to make strikes. An additional weight factor involves adjusting the weight to the left or right of the ball's center. This weight adjustment is done by a ball driller with the precise recommendation of a bowling pro who has analyzed your bowling style. The whole process is rather complicated, and you shouldn't attempt to have your ball weighted unless your average is 180 plus for men or 160 plus for women and you have access to a knowledgeable pro.

Basic Grips

As mentioned earlier, there are three basic grips: conventional, semifingertip, and full-fingertip (see figure 28). In conventional grip, the middle and ring fingers

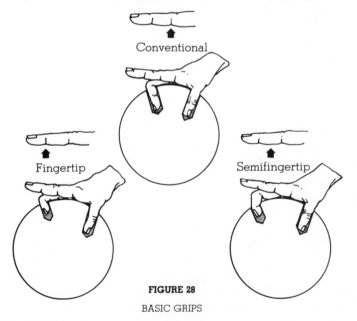

FIGURE 28

BASIC GRIPS

are inserted up to about the second knuckle. When you get to be an advanced bowler, you may want to try a semi- or full-fingertip grip, as these tend to increase the hooking characteristics of your ball. Considerable strength is needed to master these grips as your fingers are not inserted very far into the ball. For the semifingertip grip, your fingertips are inserted into the finger holes just past the first knuckle. Your fingers go in only to the first knuckle for the full-fingertip grip.

As you try new and more advanced techniques, your game average can actually drop for a time. But be patient and stick with your new skills. Gradually you will become a better bowler, and your greater sense of accomplishment and personal satisfaction will make all that practice worthwhile.

INDEX

85

The pin diagram (right side):

7 8 9 10
4 5 6
2 3
1

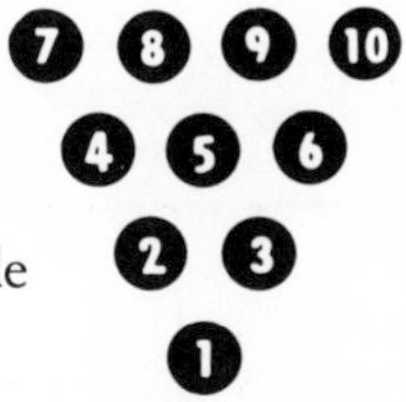

Strike Ball, 5-8 Spare, 1-2-5 Spare, 1-2-9 Spare

1. Place your right foot on the dot at the right side of the approach area.
2. Point toes toward 1–3 pocket.
3. Roll ball over the second diamond from the right side of the lane. If you roll a hook, your starting position will be three or four boards to the left of the first dot.

Five Pin

1. Line up for strike ball.
2. Roll ball over second diamond from the right. Hook-ball bowlers will have to move left one board from the strike position.

Two Pin, 1-2-4-7 Spare, 2-8 Spare

1. Move two boards to the right of your strike position.
2. Roll ball over the second diamond from the right into 1–2 pocket.

Ten Pin

1. Place left foot on last board on the left side of the lane.
2. Move four boards to your right.
3. Point toes toward 10 pin.
4. Roll ball over third diamond from the right side of the lane. If you roll a hook, start from the last board on the left side of the lane.

Six Pin, 6-10 Spare, 6-9-10 Spare, 3-6-10 Spare, 9-10 Spare, 3-10 Split

1. Move right one board from your position for the 10-pin pickup.
2. Roll ball over third diamond from the right side of the lane.

Seven Pin

1. Place your right foot on the last board on the right side of the lane.
2. Move four boards to your left.
3. Point your toes at the 7 pin.
4. Roll ball over third diamond from the right side of the lane. If you roll a hook, start eight boards from the right side of the lane.

Four Pin, 4-7 Spare, 4-7-8 Spare, 2-4-7 Spare, 7-8 Spare, 2-7 Split

1. Move left one board from your position for the 7-pin pickup.
2. Roll ball over third diamond from the right side of the lane.

QUICK REFERENCE SHEET FOR SPOT BOWLING (LEFT-HANDERS)

7 8 9 10
4 5 6
2 3
1

Strike Ball, 5-9 Spare, 1-3-5 Spare, 1-3-8 Spare

1. Place your left foot on the dot at the left side of the approach area.
2. Point toes toward 1-2 pocket.
3. Roll ball over the second diamond from the left side of the lane. If you roll a hook, your starting position will be three or four boards to the right of the first dot.

Five Pin

1. Line up for strike ball.
2. Roll ball over second diamond from the left. Hook-ball bowlers will have to move right one board from the strike position.

Three Pin, 1-3-6-10 Spare, 3-9 Spare

1. Move two boards to the left of your strike position.
2. Roll ball over the second diamond from the right into 1-3 pocket.

Ten Pin

1. Place left foot on last board on the left side of the lane.
2. Move four boards to your right.
3. Point toes toward 10 pin.
4. Roll ball over third diamond from the left side of the lane. If you roll a hook, start eight boards from the left side of the lane.

Six Pin, 6-10 Spare, 6-9-10 Spare, 3-6-10 Spare, 9-10 Spare, 3-10 Split

1. Move right one board from your position for the 10-pin pickup.
2. Roll ball over third diamond from the left side of the lane.

Seven Pin

1. Place your right foot on the last board on the right side of the lane.
2. Move four boards to your left.
3. Point your toes toward the 7 pin.
4. Roll ball over third diamond from the left side of the lane. If you roll a hook, start from the last board on the right side of the lane.

Four Pin, 4-7 Spare, 4-7-8 Spare, 2-4-7 Spare, 2-7 Split

1. Move left one board from your position for the 7-pin pickup.
2. Roll ball over third diamond from the left side of the lane.

89